On t.. Move

An information book by
Pratima Mitchell

Nelson

Thomas Nelson and Sons Ltd
Nelson House   Mayfield Road
Walton-on-Thames   Surrey
KT12 5PL   UK

Nelson Blackie
Wester Cleddens Road
Bishopbriggs
Glasgow
G64 2NZ   UK

Thomas Nelson Australia
102 Dodds Street
South Melbourne
Victoria 3205   Australia

Nelson Canada
1120 Birchmount Road
Scarborough   Ontario
MIK 5G4   Canada

Illustrated by Chris Hahner, Jane Fanner-Hoskin, Jeanette Venter
Photographs by Jane Fanner-Hoskin pp. 30, 31, 35, 40/41, 42, 43, 47
Karoki Lewis pp. 11, 13, 14, 18, 20, 21, 22, 26;
Panos Pictures: p. 9; Peter Barker p. 10; Barbara Class p. 34;
David Constantine pp. 15, 19, 28; Glenn Edwards p. 16; J. Holmes pp. 8, 27;
Chris Stowers p. 25

First published by Thomas Nelson and Sons Ltd 1996
I(T)P Thomas Nelson is an International Thomson Publishing Company
I(T)P is used under licence

ISBN 0-17-401291-8

Printed in China

Contents

On the move

Most of us are *on the move* each day.
We go to school. We go to work.
We go out to play. We visit friends.
We go to the shops.
We might even go on holiday!

5

Before we travel anywhere we have to decide **how** we will get there. To make that choice we need to think carefully about questions like these:

- Do we have to go a long way?
- Do we have to get there quickly?
- Do we have heavy things to carry?
- Do we have to go with somebody?

We might also need to ask:

- Is it expensive to travel this way?
- Is it safe to travel this way?
- Is it comfortable to travel this way?

We also need to think about whether this method of transport is 'friendly to the environment':

- Does it cause pollution to travel this way?

For short journeys we can walk or cycle using our legs.

For longer journeys we can travel in a car or go by bus or by train.

For very long journeys we can fly by plane or travel by boat.

Nowadays cars, buses, trains, boats and planes mean that people can make longer journeys more quickly and move heavy goods more easily. But cars, buses, trains, boats and planes are all driven by engines that use fuel to make them go. Fuel costs money. It causes pollution. If we can travel together in a vehicle like a bus or a train we can share the cost and reduce pollution.

Motor vehicles are a fast and convenient way to travel – we can reach anywhere in the country that is on a road. More and more roads and motorways are being built. Our towns and cities are full of cars and lorries.

In many countries of the world there are still lots of different types of transport to be found. Pakistan is one of these countries. In Pakistan motor vehicles have not replaced the strong animals that pull carts, and men can still be seen pedalling and pulling vehicles. We will look at some of these in **Part I**.

In **Part 2** we will be looking at a canal boat called the *Ipswich*. In the days before trains and lorries, narrowboats, like the *Ipswich*, were pulled along by horses and used to float heavy goods along the waterways of England.

Part I   On the move in Pakistan

- Look carefully at the photographs on the next three pages.

The photographs on these two pages show busy street scenes in two Pakistani cities – Suukur and Karachi.

This photograph shows a busy street scene in London, the capital city of Great Britain. You might have spotted some differences. In the photographs of Karachi:

- there are more scooters.
- there are more people pedalling cycles.
- there are carriages and carts pulled by animals.

Let us look more closely at some of the different ways of getting on the move in Karachi. Let us see and hear some of the sights and sounds of the crowded street scenes.

On the move – by cycle rickshaw

- How do you usually get to school each morning?
- Do you walk or ride a bike?
- Do you go by bus?
- Do you go by car?

If you lived in Karachi, you might travel to school in a box *rickshaw* like the one in this picture:

This unusual school bus is really a very big tricycle – a bike with three wheels – with a light wooden box, specially made to carry children, built on to the back of it.

Inside the wooden cabin are two benches. Six or seven small children sit on the benches. It's a tight squeeze. They sit closely together, but there isn't enough room for their school bags or water bottles! The bags and bottles are hung outside the little cabin. In the cold winter months it is nice and warm inside, but it is very stuffy and sticky in the hot summer weather.

A cycle rickshaw like this one is friendly to the environment. It does not need petrol and it does not cause pollution. It is cheap to run. But there is one problem. It isn't very safe in the middle of heavy traffic. If a bigger, heavier vehicle bumped into it, then the driver at the front or the children inside could be hurt.

Cycle rickshaws are a very popular way to travel short distances in towns in Pakistan.

Here is a rickshaw stand. It is just like a taxi rank. The rickshaw men are waiting for customers. They do not have meters to tell the passengers the cost of their fare. They tell their customers how much they will charge for the journey.

Often the customers will try to bargain with the rickshaw man. They will haggle about how much money he should charge them. If he says the journey will cost ten *rupees*, then the customer will say, 'I'll only pay eight rupees.'

The rickshaw man will then say, 'Make it nine rupees and hop on. That's my last offer!'

Ladies with their shopping bags, families going to the cinema, men who are late for work, grannies with tired legs, all like to take a rickshaw.

A cycle rickshaw can carry two adults, but parents sometimes carry children on their laps.

When it rains the hood at the back can go up and the passengers stay dry. But the rickshaw man has no shelter from the sun or the rain. Pushing the pedals is tiring because there are no gears.

The rickshaw man sounds his bell to warn other road users to get out of the way. But as he cannot go very fast, he is not a danger in crowded narrow streets.

The hubs and hoods are decorated with brightly painted flowers and patterns.

As well as people, cycle rickshaws can carry loads that are bulky, but not too heavy, such as packages and tyres. Sugarcane can also be transported by cycle rickshaw.

A stick of sugarcane is marked in sections like bamboo. The skin is straw coloured with green streaks. It is smooth and hard and shiny. If you peel off the skin with a sharp knife, you can chew the sugarcane. Sugarcane is squeezed in a machine. The sweet juice is very good to drink in the summer.

Sometimes a rickshaw is pulled by man-power.
This is how a rickshaw man pulls a heavy load.

On the move – by motor rickshaw

The motor rickshaws, or three-wheelers, are even more popular than the cycle rickshaws. They are also called 'phut-phuts' because of the sound made by the small engine of the scooter.

The man driving the motor rickshaw has a scooter to do the hard work for him. Up to six people can sit in the cab, and the scooter pulls them along.

It is much faster than a cycle rickshaw, but that makes it more dangerous.

It is driven by diesel oil and is very noisy. It causes pollution in cities.

The roof is made of plastic cloth and there is a small window in the back of the cab. The body of the cab is painted with flower patterns and slogans like, 'Have a nice Day'. Sometimes the rickshaw man decorates his three-wheeler with tinsel and ribbons which make it look bright and cheerful.

On the move – by scooter

Because cars are more expensive to buy and more expensive to run, more families have scooters than cars in Pakistan. Whole families can travel on a small scooter, with Dad driving in front. Only the driver has to wear a helmet.

Scooters are useful in traffic jams. They are small and can nip in and out of heavy traffic. They are quick and do not use a lot of fuel. But it is difficult to carry any luggage on a scooter, and it is not a very safe way to get around. There is no protection for the scooter driver or his passengers.

On the move – by bike

Bikes have to be sturdy to take all kinds of heavy loads on city streets and bumpy country roads. In Pakistan bikes have heavy frames and no gears which makes them tiring to pedal.

The milkman delivers milk by bike.

He milks his cows and buffaloes at dawn. Then he pours the creamy milk from the buckets into tin milk-cans.

Clatter-clatter, clang clang go the milk-cans as he cycles down the road early in the morning.

Bikes are used as shops on wheels. Just think, the 'shopkeeper' doesn't have to pay any rent and he can take his shop to the best places for finding customers.

This basket seller carries his goods all over the city. He cries out in a loud voice, 'Baskets, who wants my baskets?' He needs a loud voice and strong lungs and he gets very thirsty. He would save his voice if he could use a tape-recorder!

He has laundry baskets, waste-paper baskets and also stools and straw mats. He even sells bookcases and tables made from cane and straw.

Cafés too are on the move. This mobile café is a large wooden platform on four wheels.

The café owner is frying sizzling hot potato cakes on a small oil stove.

He calls out to people going by: 'Stop and buy some! Stop and buy some!'

His customers are eating a quick lunch of potato cakes, curry and rice, all served on a dried leaf for a plate.

- Potato cakes are easy to make. Ask your teacher or another adult to help you make some.

  Wash your hands first!

Ingredients

  115 grams of cooked potatoes

  30 grams of plain flour

  15 grams of melted butter

  Salt and pepper

  Cooking oil

  A frying pan

  A wooden board and a rolling pin.

Mash the potatoes. Add flour, butter, salt and pepper. Knead into a smooth dough.

Grease your palms. Take pieces of dough about the size of a ping-pong ball and roll them into balls.

Grease a wooden board, and then place each ball onto it and roll them out until they are about 1 ½ cm thick.

Put a teaspoon of oil into the frying pan and place it on a medium heat. When the oil is hot, place the potato round in it. Put a half teaspoon of oil on top of the round, turn upside down and fry.

When both sides are fried to a nice golden colour, take out the potato cake and eat with sauce. Delicious!

On the move – in horse and bullock carts

Horse carts

For longer journeys and for heavier loads, horse carts are very useful.

They are not cheap to run. The horse needs food and shoes. The rubber tyres on the cart have to be replaced when they get worn out.

But a horse cart will not cause pollution. The horse dung can be used for manure. If horse dung is mixed with earth and straw, it can be used as food for plants. Manure makes vegetables and fruit grow bigger and stronger.

Horse carts carry bricks and other materials to building sites. They can also be used to carry a lot of passengers.

Another kind of horse cart is called a *tonga*.

Two people ride in front and two behind. The seat has springs and it is quite comfortable to ride in a tonga. There is still room near the passengers' feet to take some luggage.

A tonga is handy when you get off a bus or a train. After a long journey you can hire a tonga to take you home.

The horse goes clip-clop, clip-clop. The bells on the harness go jingle-jangle, jingle jangle. 'Hup hup,' cries the tonga man to his horse.

Bullock carts
On the rough tracks and roads of the countryside the best kind of vehicle is a bullock cart.

Bullocks are valuable animals and their owners take good care of them. Bullocks are strong and good-natured, but they travel very slowly.

On the move – by truck

The strongest carriers of all are big, snub-nosed trucks. They carry goods to all parts of the country.

The trucks are painted in bright colours: orange, green, blue and red.

Truck drivers paint slogans on the backs of their trucks. 'Hello' and 'Tata' are greetings which are seen on every truck. Their sides and front are painted with roses, scenery and other pictures.

Sometimes the truckdriver fits a loudspeaker on to his vehicle. People along the way can share his taste in music. Trucks always have very loud horns which play tunes.

When they hear a truck coming, cyclists and bullock carts quickly get out of the way. Trucks go very fast and often cause accidents. They are the cheapest way to transport goods over a long distance. But they give out thick, black exhaust fumes that are not good for the environment.

Since truckdrivers sometimes have to spend many nights on the road far from home, they sleep at wayside inns called *dhabas*. They usually spend the night on a hammock, out in the open, under the starts.

They can also get a hot meal at the inn. A typical menu would be rice, *chapattis*, *dal*, vegetable curry, meat curry or chicken curry. The truck drivers wash their meal down with cold fizzy drinks.

Part 2 On the move in a narrowboat

On the canal – the Ipswich

The *Ipswich* is a canal boat. It is about ten times as long as it is wide. You can see why such canal boats got their name narrowboats.

The *Ipswich* is one of the most beautifully painted canal boats in England. Jane lives on the boat with her husband Vincent and her son Tom. Jane has used bottle green as the main colour, but she has also used four other colours to decorate it: yellow, red, blue and white. She has decorated it with simple patterns and with detailed pictures too.

Roses and castles

The top of the tiller, which was used to steer the boat, has a simple pattern. It is painted in red, yellow, white and green stripes. But behind the cabin doors on each side, Jane has painted a pattern of three roses surrounded by four white daisies.

 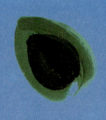 

1   Paint a circle about 3–4 cm in diameter.
2   Add highlights.
3   Paint a black circle in the centre of the round highlight.
4   Add leaves around the rose circle.

To paint the leaves
5   Two brush strokes in medium green.
6   Fill the centre of the leaf in dark green.
7   Add brown to the bottom of the leaf.
8   Add leaf 'veins' with a single stroke of the brush.
9   A different sort of leaf with black veins and white edges.

Roses
10 Practise the brush strokes for the petals.
11 Add the petals to your roses.
12 The completed rose
13 Put it all together!

Above the roses she has painted a castle. The picture looks like a castle from a fairy tale. It has high towers with turrets, and flags, called pennants, flying in the wind. On the outside of the cabin is another, larger, painting of a castle.

Roses and castles can be found on nearly all canal boats. But you can also see similar designs decorating other types of vehicles.

Places to Visit

If you would like to find out more about canals and narrowboats, here is a list of places to visit:

Black Country Museum,
Tipton Road Dudley,
West Midlands DY1 4SQ

Telephone: 0121-557-9643

Boat Museum,
Dockyard Road,
Ellesmere Port,
Cheshire L65 4EF

Telephone: 0151-355 5017

Canal Museum,
Canal Street,
Nottingham NG1 7ET

Telephone: 01602 598835

Canal Museum,
Stoke Bruerne,
Towcester,
Northamptonshire NN12 7SE

Telephone: 01604 862229

London Canal Museum,
12/13 New Wharf Road,
Kings Cross,
London N1 9RT

Telephone: 0171-713-0836

National Waterways
Museum,
Llanthony Warehouse,
The Docks,
Gloucester GL1 2EH

Telephone: 01452 307009

There are other, smaller, canal museums at Devizes, Wiltshire; Llangollen, Clwyd; Shardlow, Derbyshire; and Welshpool, Powys.